Looking Back Into Yesterday

Emily Lorlene Albertha Malcolm

My Country Turks and Caicos

Sponsored by the department of Culture, TCI

Contents

Acknowledgements	5
Foreword	6
Introduction	7
I. A role to play	10

My Country Turks and Caicos:

Places of Interest
II. The Salt Islands	14
III. The Salt Ponds	16
IV. Conch Ground	19

Things to See
V. My Country's Fruits	22
VI. My Mango Seed Doll	24
VII. Our native Christmas Tree (TCI dialect)	27
VIII. Our native Christmas Tree	29
IX. De Conch	32
X. De Masses	34

Pastimes
XI. Hopscotch	39
XII. She's fishing	40
XIII. Bush Picnics	43
XIV. Ring Games	44
XV. Kite Flying	46
XVI. Top Spinning	48
XVII. Marbles	50
XVIII. Skipping	53
XIX. Can we go in town? ... We goin in town!	54

Local Cuisine
XX. Chocolate lumps	58
XXI. Fried fish row	60
XXII. Home-made Ice Cream	62

XXIII. Pear Bush	64
XXIV. Preserves We Made	67
XXV. Bread Making	68

Traditions

XXVI. Set de tubs! De rain comin!	72
XXVII. The Sea Horse	74
XXVIII. The Donkey Cart	76
XXIX. Bay Tansy	78
XXX. The Oil Stove	80
XXXI. Haiti boat in	83
XXXII. Aunty Flossy's Date Tree	84
XXXIII. On de Bench	86
XXXIV. Gathering Firewood	89
XXXV. Drought	90
XXXVI. Scale	92
XXXVII. Dried Conch	94

Community

XXXVIII. Community Policing	98
XXXIX. Our Tasks	100
XL. Recognizing Achievement, Promoting Excellence	102
XLI. Exploring New Possibilities	104
XLII. Looking Back	106

Acknowledgements

This book is dedicated to my mother, Iris Aslene Lightbourne-Malcolm affectionately called 'Tit", whose love for Cultural Heritage, has motivated and inspired me to write.

I give thanks to the Lord Almighty for the years He has given me and kept me in the field of my chosen career, Education. I do believe that God will use this book far above our greatest imagination for the purpose of educating this and future generations about aspects of the history of the Turks and Caicos Islands. Thank You, Lord for the realization of this book.

I give God all the praise and glory for the talents with which I am blessed and the ability to capture history in poetry form. My heartfelt thanks and gratitude to the Hon. Karen Malcolm, former Minister of Education, Youth, Culture, Library Services, Gender Affairs and Social Development, Permanent Secretary Mr. Wesley Clerveaux and Director of Culture, Miss Ludwina Fulford, financial assistance for printing from Colin Kihnke's South Caicos Heritage Foundation, Dr. Christian Buys, Dayna Higgs, Tatiana Hendfield, Evgeniia Smolentseva for her awesome illustrations. Your support in advancing our cultural heritage through this book is hereby recognized and greatly appreciated. Your assistance made this publication possible.

I acknowledge and say special thanks for editorial assistance in reading the content, so that we could present history through poetry in its right context:
Gladys Kennedy
Noreane Williams-McKoy
Candianne Williams
Maria Clare
Bishop George Fulford

Thank you, my friends for your encouragement and support.

Thanks to my brother Coven Malcolm, who responded to every call, understood my concern in getting the facts about various topics correct and who assisted and encouraged me on this journey.

Foreword

This book takes you, the reader into the Cultural Heritage of the Turks and Caicos Islands. It depicts the life I knew and that of many others when we were children. It describes acts of love and socializing for adults and children. It is hoped that it is motivation to learn as much as one can about events that happened in the Turks and Caicos Islands many years ago, although some are still current today. The stories are referenced through poetry of its people and their way of life.

It is my hope that by sharing this information that readers - young and old, around the world will learn about our country and aspects of its history.

I would like for our senior citizens and adults who can relate to the stories told herein to understand the importance of talking about what life was like years ago and how it has change today to their grandchildren and others. It is very important that the Cultural Heritage of one's country be kept alive. Talking about it can do that too.

The way of expression will be criticized, but that is ok, as an educator I learnt, practiced and supported the efforts of all my students when they expressed themselves. I wrote how I know that we, Turks and Caicos Islanders thought, still think, speak and so this is my way of expression.

May all who read recognize the richness of Turks and Caicos Islands, Cultural Heritage, learn some fact about events which happened in the various islands and get motivated to experience life throughout the islands.

Introduction

Preserving Cultural Heritage

Cultural heritage affirms a nation's identity as a people. It creates a framework for the preservation of "Culture" and "Heritage". These are properties of culture, values and traditions that are passed down from previous generations. Cultural heritage implies a shared bond to our past, present and the future. It represents our history and our identity.

Tangible Culture (Material elements) that one can see and touch and have cultural significance and historical value, does not limit cultural heritage. These are worthy of preservation for future generations. Intangible Culture (Immaterial elements), are traditions, oral history, performing arts, social practices, traditional craftsmanship, representations, rituals, knowledge and skills. The cultural heritage of any nation is unique and very important. Culture and its heritage reflect and shape values, beliefs, and aspirations, thereby defining a people's national identity. They are the identity that introduces that nation to the world.

Immaterial elements give one the knowledge and skills to produce traditional crafts, folklore, traditions and language. Regardless of what they are, these things form part of a natural heritage of living expressions from our ancestors that have been passed on to our descendants. This heritage requires active effort on our part in order to safeguard it. Its significance, value and the emotion within us, should cause us to feel as though we belong to a country, a tradition, or a way of life. Their preservation demonstrates recognition of the necessity of the past and of the things that tell its story. It is therefore important for us to preserve Turks and Caicos Islands heritage and traditions because it keeps our integrity as a people.

It is of great importance that one understands and shows respect for both tangible and intangible elements in relation to indigenous culture of one's country. Without knowledge and practice of one's country cultural heritage, formulating anything different does not have the same meaning. The best way to preserve one's cultural heritage, whatever it may be, is to share it with others.

Why is Cultural Heritage Important?

The importance of intangible cultural heritage is the wealth of knowledge and skills that are transmitted through it from one generation to the next. The social and economic value of knowledge is relevant for minority groups and for mainstream social groups within one's country. It is also important for development as the country develops.

> **A country's cultural heritage is important because it highlights the recognition of international qualifications for its preservation and integration for immigrant receiving countries.**

How do we preserve heritage, tradition and culture in culturally diverse societies?

Intangible cultural heritage is an important factor in maintaining cultural diversity in the face of growing globalisation. It is necessary for one to understand the intangible cultural heritage of different communities. This helps with intercultural dialogue and encourages mutual respect for other people ways of life. There is the risk that certain elements of intangible cultural heritage could die out or disappear without help or assistance. Safeguarding is about the transferring of knowledge, skills and meaning.

How can Turks and Caicos, safeguard and manage a heritage that is constantly changing and part of 'living culture' without freezing or trivialising it?

To safeguard our cultural heritage, we must focus on the processes involved in transmitting, or communicating intangible cultural heritage from generation to generation.

Preservation of culture and heritage through education

The role of media is very important in preserving culture and heritage. Digital storage plays a major role in the preservation of cultural heritage. It is the trend for the future. It enables the sharing of cultural and historical heritage around the world. Sustainability in the preservation of tangible and intangible cultural heritage through education should be encouraged. It is a way of how they can be safeguarded. The appreciation of cultural heritage should be communicated through an integrated education approach.

Protecting culture and heritage

The role of the Turks and Caicos society in preserving heritage and culture is the active involvement of its people and good practice on experiences in securing data from generations around cultural heritage, and their impact on its healthy development. This is the best way to safeguard heritage and create opportunities for human and economic development.

In order to protect and keep Turks and Caicos cultural heritage alive, tangible and intangible cultural heritage must remain relevant to our culture and be regularly practiced and learnt within the communities of each island, thus the country at large and between generations.

The protection of cultural property is an old problem. One of the most frequently recurring issues in protecting cultural heritage is the difficult relationship between the interests of the individual and the community, the balance between private and public rights.

Stories are also important and may have significance to broader areas of a country. The recounting and transmission of stories ensures that designs and processes for representing stories of country are carefully managed and protected.

Cultural heritage is also the result of a selection process: a process of memory and awareness that characterizes every human society constantly engaged in choosing—for both cultural and political reasons—what is worthy of being preserved for future generations and what is not.

Cultural heritage passed down to us from our parents must be preserved for the benefit of all. In an era of globalization, cultural heritage helps us to remember our cultural diversity, and its understanding develops mutual respect and renewed dialogue amongst different cultures.

It is important to know, learn and understand the concept of Cultural Heritage. It is my hope that the poems written in this book will enable generations to recall, ask questions and talk about Turks and Caicos cultural heritage.

I
A ROLE TO PLAY

Every Turks and Caicos Islander,
you have a role to play
Educate your children,
Our visitors ..... our guests about yesterday.
Remember what you lived and
The stories you were told.
Today, they are part of history
Even though you may think they are old.

Sand, sea and sun
Is much fun,
But many of our guests
Want more than that.

Our Cultural Heritage should be on display,
Talk about what makes
Turks and Caicos great.
There is much to learn about the place
We call home:
The way we lived,
The food we ate,
Forms of recreation, our clothes and footwear ----

Did I hear, 'Whampos, Pusses'?
Yes, so true,
Don't feel ashamed,
Your parents, grandparents
Mine,
Would have worn them too.

Boat building was such a great skill,
But a boat launch, greater still.
The excitement, the merry making,
Oh, this was fun,
But the final act, was to burst
That bottle of rum.

'Heritage House', at the Museum,
In the Village at Grace Bay
Gives the real experience.
Be their guests
So, children and youths too can share in ---
Our Cultural Heritage journeys.

It's my story,
Your story,
Our stories,
And that of future generations ------
Turks and Caicos history.

***

MY COUNTRY PLACES OF INTEREST

II
THE SALT ISLANDS

The 'Salt Islands'
They numbered three –
Grand Turk, South Caicos and Salt Cay.

The Bermudians came in the 1670's
And for more than three hundred years
Operated the Salt Industry.

Ponds were built into pans
Trenched with ballast rocks from Bermuda.
These in schooners came
Since they would have had trouble
Returning empty.

Slaves as salt rakers
Had no other choice than to brave the heat
Or be flogged.

They raked the salt into mounds
To be loaded onto mule carts
Taken to designated depots
To be bagged
By the women.

Later in life
Salt was put in barrels
And moved from the ponds to the dock
In mule, horse or donkey carts.

Then came the time
When salt: 'White Gold'
Became the main industry.
Turks Island salt
Made history …..
It had a reputation for its good quality.

In 1883,
A silver medal won.
Amsterdam International Exhibits.
In 1891,
A diploma awarded,
General excellence of salt exhibits.
Jamaica International Exhibits.
1976,
Salt industry ended.

***

III
THE SALT PONDS

The salt ponds are now
Remains of the salt industry,
So, they help us to recall history.

The slaves did an excellent job
Guided by the Bermudians,
To trench saltwater,
Channelled through canals from the sea,
To every pond
As the water ran free.

Solar power windmills,
Placed here and there
Played their role
In helping to execute
The Bermudians plan.
They ensured that
Water flowed from pond to pond,
Because large production
Was in great demand.

Look at the ponds;
Pretty in pink,
Transformed by the ocean,
Sea water blue,
In a few weeks

Just you wink or blink
You will see a blanket of snow
White
Like diamonds glistening so bright.
It is no wonder, we were told
The fruits of the labourer were
Known as White Gold!

For the people of the islands,
It was seasoning salt,
Preserver for fish, pork, beef and more
Keeping the ice cream freezer going
Was the best of all.

The last of the salt left in the pond
Was raked up, taken out
And left so that the pickle drained off.
It turned hard and grey
And the name it got was 'Scale'.
This was put on the roads,
And flattened to make a smooth surface.

The beautiful hues of water
Seen in the ponds
Was no indication
What the workers endured.
Working in pickle, brine
And just mere salt.

The shiny, glittering glare
From the sun on the salt,
Impaired the vision
Of them All.
And so were blisters on their feet
And
Sweat became salt.
This was the fate of All.

***

IV
CONCH GROUND

Conch Ground, the hot spot
By the seaside, where
Fishermen leave every morning to go to sea.
On their return,
Off load their catch
Fish, lobster, conch or turtle
And sell to processing plants or individuals
If that's their intention,
Then tie-up their boats
And take some home for the family's consumption.

Conch Ground, the place where people meet
To eat, at Darrel's restaurant
Or buy a few drinks
Socializing with friends.
A game of dominoes
Is sure to be played
Even if the players
Came on errand to get a meal.

Conch Ground, the place
You'll hear the latest news!
Voices which seem so silent
Often speak their mind and give their opinion.
Conch Ground,
That's where you shop
At Seaview Supermarket
For all your grocery needs and gasoline.

Conch Ground, the place to drop your line
And catch some fish.
Wait around and you're sure to get
Fresh conch.
Conch Ground, the place to be
If you want to know what's happening
In my community!

***

THINGS TO SEE

V
MY COUNTRY'S FRUITS

My country's fruits
Are not much different
From those around the world.
Yes, fewer and not a large variety
Yet just as nice and tasty.

Tamarind, guinep, pomegranate
And guavas,
Grow in the wild.
Sappadilly,
Garden cherries and sugar apples
Can also be in great supply.

Banana, coconut,
Papaw and parpoon
Grow in abundance too.

Mango, soursop and pineapple
Are newcomers to the list.

On every island
Crops can grow,
Although
Some soil will need enrichment
A good crop to produce.
One can have
One's own favourite fruit
In abundance from one's own yard.
Grow your fruits,
Eat them,
Make drinks and smoothies too!

Use leaves from
The guava and soursop tree
To make
Some nice, rich bush tea.

Fruits are great health foods
So, grow what you can
On your own land.

***

VI
MY MANGO SEED DOLL

I won't lick this one clean.
I'll use it to make my doll,
With the meat that's left on my seed.
I'll have hair to comb
And beautify.

She will be the best one yet,
She has more hair to plait.
I will dress her up
Better than the rest.
Let me get busy
Designing her first dress.

Before that happens,
I will clean her up,
Put her aside
Just to make sure
That no one picks her up.

I will wash my seed
Until the juice disappears,
Put it to dry
Where it cannot be seen
Then dress it up
Like a 'Beauty Queen'.

Where are my scraps?
Oh! Beautiful -----
These will make some stylish clothes.
These are bright colours
Bold and lavish
My doll will have lots
And lots of clothes.

Now that you are dry my seed -----
You will become my doll baby,
I will make you prettier than all the others,
With
Fancy hair styles
Ribbons
And wraps.
You will always be
My favourite doll.

***

VII
OUR NATIVE CHRISTMAS TREE
(Turks and Caicos dialect)

You goin in de bush?
For wha?
To ge Christmas Trees!
Oh my! Gurl, I faget bout dat.
But tiene time to ge dem now.
I know, but we wan one.
So, wen you go, dun faget.

We goin in de bush Satday,
You still need de tree?
How you mean,
We still waitin on dat.
I can come too?

Yall smell dat?
Boy dess a nice smell.
Dess how de Christmas tree dem smell.
Now, des Christmas. Yeah.
But watch out for de prickles,
Dey can stick, and wen dey juke you
Dat dis hut.
So, how we goin ge-tit den?

Ge de cutlist, we gata chop it down.
How we ga carry it?
In de donkey cart.
Wha ga happen to we?
What you mean?
How we ga ge back in town?
Walk behind de donkey cart.

Our journey through de shrubby trees
Gave my arms and legs
Some burning scorches
And even though it hut so bad
I was glad, my Christmas Tree---- I had.
Wen we ge back to de road,
I was anxious to ge back home.

We walked de dusty, rocky road
Behind de donkey cart
Till we ge to our yard.
De trees were taken from de cart
And put outside de door,
Den we ge de bucket and things:
Rocks ------, big and small
Sand,
Christmas paper and all.

Dis sticky green tree wit its prickles and
Sweet, strong fragrance,
Has already changed my mood
To joyous and excited!

Iie!!! ... Iie!!! ... Iie!!!
Dis stick hard,
But I mus ge my tree in de right part.
I'll pull it and
Push it till I ge it in place
Cause dis goin make my Christmas Day!

Dere you are ----
In de corner chosen
And dere you'll stay
Until after Christmas Day!

Look at de beautiful clothes
Decorating de tree!
Everyone who comes to my house
Will see wha Santa Claus
Brought me!

Tank you Lord for de few
Tin toys dat came from Haiti.
I so glad that I ga my doll from Inagua
And Santa was good to me.

***

VIII
OUR NATIVE CHRISTMAS TREE

Are you going in the bush?
For what?
To get Christmas trees!
Oh my! Girl I forgot about that
But it is not time to get them yet.
I know, but we would like to have one
Whenever you go,
So, when you do, do not forget

We are going in the bush on Saturday,
Do you still need the tree?
How do you mean?
We are waiting on that.
Can I come too?

Do you smell that?
Boy! That is a nice smell.
That is how the Christmas trees smell
Now this is Christmas!
Yeah, but look out for the prickles,
They do stick.
When they do
The stick hurts very much.

So how are we going to get it then?
Get the cutlass, we will have to chop it down.
How are we going to carry it?
In the donkey cart.
What is going to happen to us?
How are we going to get back to town?
We will walk behind the donkey cart ……

Our journey through the shrubby trees
Gave my arms and legs
Some burning scorches.
When we reached the main road
I was relieved, but not for long.

We walked the dusty, rocky road
Behind the donkey cart
Until we got to our yard.
The tree was taken from the cart
And put outside the dining room door.

We were so excited to put up our tree!
So, we got the bucket and things:
Rocks, --- big and small,
Bay sand,
Christmas paper and all.

This sticky green tree
With so many prickles, but
Sweet, strong fragrance ....,
Has put me in the Christmas mood -
Excited, happy and joyous!

Iie! Iie! Iie!
This sticks really hard,
But I must get my tree in the right part.
I'll pull it and
Push it till I get it in place
Because this is going to make my Christmas Day!

There you are ----
In the corner chosen
And there you will stay
Until long after Christmas Day!

Look at the beautiful clothes
Decorating the tree!
Everyone who comes to my house
Will see what Santa Claus
Brought for me!

Thank you, Lord for the few
Tin toys that came from Haiti.
I am so glad that I got my doll from Inagua
And Santa was good to me.

***

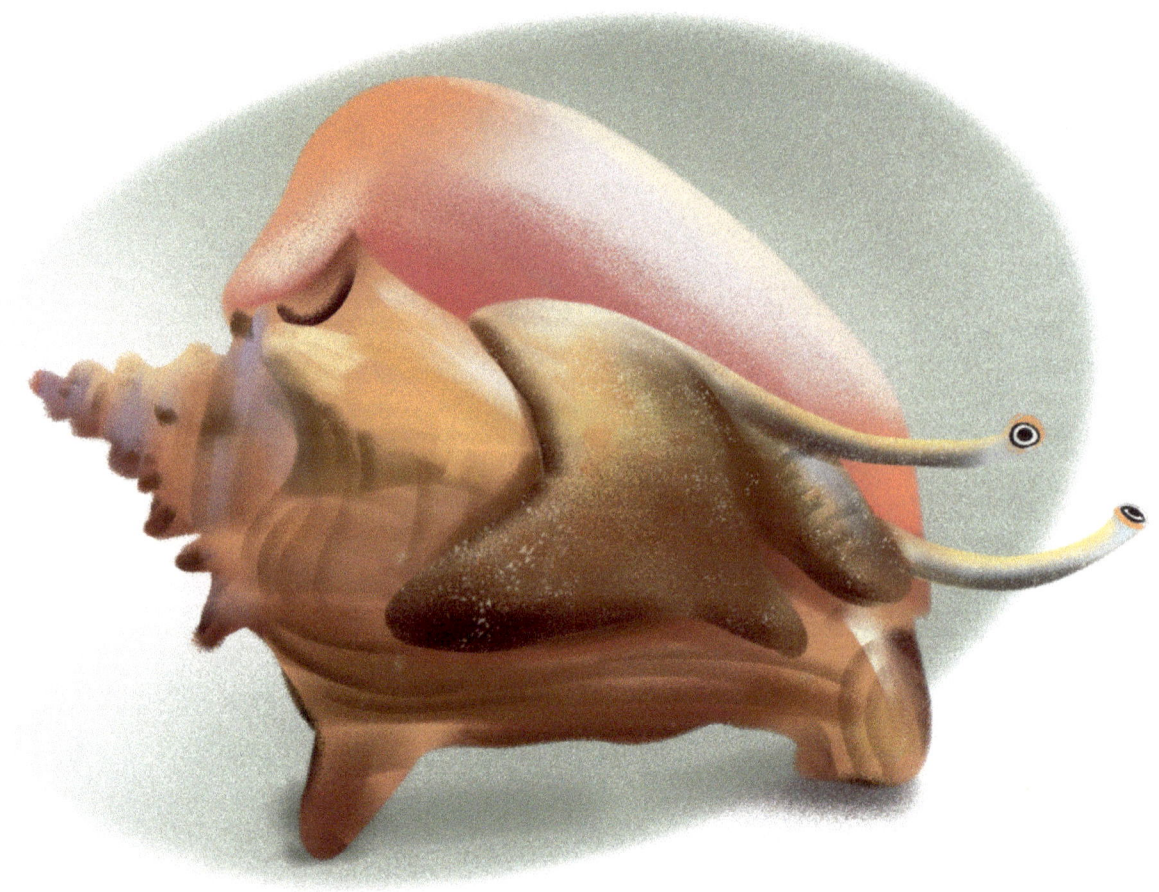

IX
DE CONCH

Wha dat?
You say conch?
Look, how it look?
Slimey ------------,
Wha dat?
You say, the gut?
That's plenty gut,
But it colourful ---------!
Pretty red, yellow, black and white.

Wha dat hard thing at de top?
You say de horn to pull it out the shell?

Looking at dat
I don know if I coulda eat it.
I wan try it though.

You say you ga some conch dishes ready?
Tell me wha you ga.
Conch Salid!
Conch Frittas!
Crack Conch!
Conch and Hominy!
And Conch and Rice!

Mmmmm ...... my mout watering!!!!!
I gotta try somethin.
Gimme the crack conch fust -----
Whoa, dis how dis taste?
Seasined, crunchy-soft and nice!
Dis taste so good,
I gotta taste all.

Well, I so glad I taste
De conch
Widout thinkin bout wha it look like.
I know I ga plenty more to eat
Cause livin in TCI
De conch dishes are considered meat.

Eat yur conch
However, you wish,
But for me ... Cracked Conch
Is de best dish.

***

X
DE MASSES

De Masses out!
De Masses out!
Dey coming down de road!
Hear de saw and de drum!
Dey comin! Dey comin!
Watch de lil children
Runnin and screaming!
Looka that one -----,
Outta bref
Makin road to ga home!

De Masses on their way to our house.
Dey reach.
I don know nobody.
These some colourful costumes.
Looka de women !
Dressed up in high heels,
Handbags and wigs of every colour
And fancy hair dos.

But voice like men.
Who dey is?
We can't tell
But dey sure represent women well!

Dey getting ready to dance now
So, bring out de money
What you got.
Put it on de groun
Dey goin dance!
Watch dis one with de burgundy wig!
Boy, she sha-shaying aye?
Looka tha one in de red high heels
Only leave for her
To broke her skinny legs.
Looka here! Looka here!
Dey want take up de money.
De Masses goin aready!
Dey goin leave now
But who goin ga de money?

***

PASTIMES

XI
HOPSCOTCH

This is good ground
To draw my 'Hopscotch'.
I'll make it big
With neat little boxes.
Put wings on either side
Of Box Number 1,
And these I'll use
Until the game I've won.

My man, will be this
BIG nail,
He'll help me win
Every game.
And when the boxes
I would have won
Stop you my friend
From moving along --------,
I'll rent for a dollar each
And with my money
I'll buy lots of sweets.

Who would like to play with me?
Come join in the fun
Let's see who can beat everyone.
That is …. Who gets the most boxes,
And makes it difficult
For players to move.
I have my skill of
How I am going to play,
The game is mine,
Watch me celebrate!

***

XII
SHE'S FISHING

Patsy went fishing.
She took her fishing lines,
Sinkers, hooks, and conch slop for bait.

She cut her bait in tiny pieces
Just big enough to tease each fishes,
Then she jammed it on the hook
And threw her line into the sea,
Ready to strike that fish
Who wants to eat?

Patiently
She stood upon the rocky cliff
And waited for a pick.
Then came that clever one
The conch bait it did prick.

That was the prick
For which she had waited:
And with a thug on her line
She saved that big red snapper
Just in time.

The slop was far from finished
The tide was flowing, and fish were biting
Time did not matter.
The catch was just getting bigger.
Fish, and more fish were all that mattered.

With the swipe of the knife
One fish became bait and
Fish were caught for each pick they did take.

***

XIII
BUSH PICNICS

Bush picnics
Were really a treat -------.
Finding shade under a shrub tree!

But then there were plenty people,
Plenty food and drink ...
SWITCHA!!!
Lime Juice and sugar
The island's notorious refreshing drink.

Everyone – men and women
Boys and girls
Chatted freely without interruptions.
There were stories, jokes ----,
Teasing and mocking of
Other persons.

That was only part of the fun,
Cause, out in the open dusty ground
Boys and girls played:
Hide and Seek,
Hopscotch,
Marbles,
Tops,
Rounders,
Skipping
And some
Just ran around.

Bush picnics in hot, dry, dusty ground
Was time shared and bought much pleasure
That today, cannot be found.

***

XIV
RING GAMES

No matter what time of day
Boys and girls came out to play
We held hands and danced around
We played ring games
Wherever cleared ground was found.
Special places were on the airport strip,
White Houses and the Parade Ground
Of course.

Moonlight nights were special treats
We would then show our motions
And not be teased.
'There's a Brown Girl in the Ring',
Just happened to be a special thing.

'Steal um Sam' and 'One in Twenty'
Were also hot on the list
But many times, we the younger ones
Never got picked.

But we kept the game going
Because others were having fun
And this pastime enabled us
To be in touched with young people
We admired so much.

***

XV
KITE FLYING

Look over there,
There are kites everywhere,
Big, small and in between.
It is kite time
And everyone wants to fly one.
Let's run along and
Join in the fun because one by one
They will be coming down.

Whose kite is that
Humming up there?
It is big and beautiful as
The rainbow's glare.
It is dancing to the feel of air,
Look!
It dips and dives as if falling in fear,
But then it bounces back and starts humming again.

Others now realize that it is
Kite Flying Day!
So, here they come to mount theirs too.
They have different sizes,
Colour and shapes.
Today's competition is going to be great.
As you can see,
There is none so far
As beautiful as
'King Over the Sea'!

From what materials
Do you think they were made?
Don't ask me,
Just ask grandpa and
He'll tell the tale.
So, get your paper, rags and sticks
Grandpa will show you the tricks.
Then you will make your kite,
Quick! Quick! Quick!

***

XVI
TOP SPINNING

That's my piece of wood
To make my top,
It's lignum vitae bark
I cut from the tree
On the hilltop.

I will cut it,
Then shape it
Just as I wish -
And sandpaper it
As smooth as
The sides of a dish.

My dad will drill the hole
In which the nail will go,
He'll hammer it in slightly
So, it will fit exactly the way it should.

After cutting it to the size
It should be
I'll use his file and a pointed
Head you'll see.

My special string will make her sing,
And boy, those guys
Will get jealous of this new thing!

The guys will be scared
When they see my new top
Cause it will be
'King' of the ground when I let her drop.

She will spin and sleep even when I pick her up.
And many boys will lose their tops
When I hit them …
As my top, I drop.

***

XVII
MARBLES

Hard glassy spheres
In different sizes with different colours,
Called marbles and a big one called Tar
Are used to play
The game of Marbles.

A group of children are out to play.
Each will choose his player and several more marbles.
A circle and a line about three feet away
Are drawn on the ground
They are needed for the game to go on.

The game begins as each put marbles in the ring,
Then one by one, stand in it and throw his player
Towards the line.
The person who goes closest to it
Plays first.

He tries to knock the marbles out of the ring
If on his first attempt, he gets one
He continues until he gets none.
Then the next person tries
And the same instruction applies
Until all players have tried.

'Knocksing', was a popular phrase
Used by players in the game.
At some point, one or sometimes all
Would bend low,
Clear a spot on the ground,
Hold his player between
His thumb and the next finger
And with a click
Release it!
This was just another way to play,
And some guys were great!
They used this skill.

This they used to remove marbles from the ring
And kill another player,
But not a Tar.
Played in the game.

To win the game
A player must collect the most marbles
Or kill the other boys' players
But cannot kill a Tar.

***

XVIII
SKIPPING

With a rope in my hand,
I will skip for as long as I can.
I can invite some friends to play
But they will have to work first
If that is Ok!
Two will turn the ends of the rope
While I skip....and only stop
When I get out.

I can also skip
All by myself,
Just by holding the ends of the rope,
Bringing it over my head
And carrying it under my feet as I jump.
This I like to do ---
But skipping with two friends
Is more fun too.

Skipping in a group
Can be funny too,
Because someone will definitely
Bump into you.
If you hold your ground
And skip your way through.

***

XIX
CAN WE GO IN TOWN? …WE GOIN IN TOWN!

It's Sunday.
Sunday School is over
And all the children and young people
Want to go to the town area to socialize.
So, we go back home to ask the question:
'Can we go in town?'
The answer would be 'Yes',
But you had to ask!

What will be happening in town?
Nothing! Nothing?
Let me say it right,
"Nothing special".
We would walk the blocks
Just laughing and talking;
Making jokes.
For us, this was fun.
Just the thought of knowing
One had permission

To go in town was exciting!
'We goin in town!'
What an awesome feeling it was?

For those who had found love,
This was their sure once a week
Courtship experience.
If not known before,
Sunday afternoon in town
Told it all.

One's next Sunday in town
Depended on whether or not
The affairs were news around town.
Just in case your girl or guy
Was not your parents' choice
Then you know that
Your visit to town on Sunday after Sunday School
Was on recess.
That meant
You aint goin in town, on
Sunday after Sunday School.

Sometimes your behaviour for the entire week
Was the determining factor as to ...
Can we go in town? .... We goin in town!

***

LOCAL CUISINE

XX
CHOCOLATE LUMPS

Chalk-lit- Lumps! Lumps! Lumps!
It's my breakfast and sometimes lunch.
It's a rainy weather treat
Eaten whenever one pleases.
It's sumptuous for any meal,
But great for cold evenings.

This chocolate mixture
Made from flour, sweet milk and cocoa
Flavoured with cinnamon,
Dried orange peel or raisins --------
Is loaded with cake -like dumplings
Delicious ------ for munching.
Mmmmmmm!

Keep those dumplings floating
Cause my appetite is in motion.
Chalk-lit- Lumps! Lumps! Lumps!

Many times,
One will ask for more,
And most times there is none for sure.
An empty pot is usually seen,
But in a short time
Another pot is cooked and ready.
Then everybody gets hungry-
All over again.
Mmmmmmmm!

The strong chocolate aroma
Again, will fill the air
Awakening appetites
For another course
Of
Chalk-lit- Lumps! Lumps! Lumps!

Keep those dumplings floating
Cause my appetite
Is in motion.
Chalk-lit- Lumps! Lumps! Lumps!

***

XXI
FRIED FISH ROW

Fish Row is the
Long, flat, grainy, yellow cluster
Of fish eggs,
Found inside the belly of
The bonefish.

What is this?
One might ask,
But don't be too quick
To say it out loud.
This delicacy may
Or will disappear!
So, if you don't know
What it is,
Keep that a secret,
Secure it so later
You can have it.

Fish Row!
Yes, it is Fish Row.
There are two of them
Because they come in pairs
So, handle them
"With care',
For they are easily broken.

Rinse with salt and water.
Season as you like,
Then dust with flour
And fry in hot deep fat.

How you eat it
Is your choice
Just have it warm
And you won't have enough!

***

XXII
HOME-MADE ICE CREAM

Home-made ice cream!
Hear the words
And taste buds go crazy....
Sunday afternoon treat
But also, any other
Social gathering.
I-c-e c-r-e-a-m!

A mixture of cream, sweet milk,
Fruit cocktail and vanilla
Poured into a freezer container,
Is set in a wooden bucket
Made especially for this mixture.

Around it, is packed
Ice, salt, ice, salt
Until it reaches the hole
In the bucket
Through which the water will fall.

On top of the container
A handle placed,
It is fastened to the bucket
To keep it in place.

Turn the handle
And the container turns too.
Go at a steady pace
This takes some time to do.
Thirty minutes or more
You will need
In order to have home-made ice cream.
The choice
Is yours -----
What is it going to be ...
A cup or a cone?

My finger-licking ice cream,
Home-made ice cream,
The best ice cream,
One will ever eat!

***

XXIII
PEAR BUSH

There it is .... Pear Bush
That prickly evergreen plant
With its green buds
Decorated with open yellow flowers.
But some are still closed
Pinkish in colour, circular in shape
With a pointed tip.

Those buds can make a tasty dish
However, you wish ------
Try buds and rice with dry conch
And plenty pigtail,
Pear bush bud soup -------
With ground provisions -

Sweet potato, cassava, eddoes and yam
But one must also include
Dry conch and plenty pigtail.
Season them well and
A mouth-watering dish you will be glad to eat.

Some islanders still
Cook those dishes even today,
There are pear bush trees in certain areas –
Called in the bush
Where people go, to cut buds
And sell them
If someone wants to buy
While others
Do it as a hobby
And give to family and friends.

The pear bush leaves, once our shampoo,
Was every Saturday task
To prepare them too.
Cut them off the tree
Remove each prickle
Then slice in two.
Use to lather the hair as if one is using shampoo.

Today it is sometimes used for
Yard decoration
A reminder of history,
But on some islands
Wild donkeys and cows treasure it as food.

***

XXIV
PRESERVES WE MADE

Of all the indigenous fruits we had
Way back then, only
Two
Were used to make preserve:
Tambrind and cherry
Were always in abundance
And we, as children made good use of them.

We climbed trees to pick tambrinds.
When we knew we had, had enough, we stopped.
We shelled, then put to boil.
The water was drained and used to make a drink,
While sugar and some baking soda
Was added to the pulp
And cooked to make tambrind preserve.

The cherries were picked in similar fashion
Although not having to climb a tree,
Were picked and boiled in far less water.
The water drained served two purposes
To make a drink and to boil into jelly.
Sugar was added to the cherries
And this was cooked until it became jelly.

We had no electricity or gas
On which to cook
But we made use of three rocks and wood.
Any wide mouth can was our pot
All we wanted
Was that tasty, nice stuff.

We ate it just like that,
And most had a belly full
Without anything else.
Today children do not make preserves
But we, the older ones
Will not let the making of them die.

***

XXV
BREAD MAKING

We had no bakeries
So almost every woman
Knew how to bake bread.
This skill was learnt during teenage years,
Society thought that, that was a woman's job.

Just about every day
But especially on Saturday,
The smell of fresh bread
Was an aroma
That got locked in your head.
Every home had someone baking bread.

The ovens were made from drums
Or wooden boxes lined with zinc or tin.

A coal stove,
Sometimes made from cast iron or tin cannisters
Gave heat to this piece of craft.

The ingredients were quite simple:
Flour, lard, yeast, sugar,
Water and salt
These were the items needed.
The yeast was mixed with water and a little sugar
And set to rise,
All other ingredients were put in a bowl
And the yeast mixture and water to make dough.
This was kneaded and
Put to rise, to double in size
And then cut in individual loaves
To rise again
In line with the top of the pan.

The stove was lit and put inside the oven to heat it.
When the loaves had risen
They were placed in the heated oven
For an hour or just a little longer.
When baked, they were removed
Taken out of the pan
And put to cool.

***

TRADITIONS

XXVI
SET DE TUBS! DE RAIN COMIN!

De sky looks pretty clear to me.

Set the tubs, the rain comin!
Set de tubs!
Put them near the house under the gutter.

A brighter blue
I can't imagine
With no rain clouds even in view.
But, she says:
Set de tubs de rain comin!

While you're at it,
Pick in de clothes
Cause de rain comin.
Now I have to take dem off
De rocks and trees

And put dem neatly in de basin.
This will make it easier to press.

De rain comin!
We gotta close-up de house.
Before dat happens
Bring in de dried fish and conch.
Hang dem in de kitchen
On de line.

Wha dat?

Outside so white
Mom, you were right
De rain aint comin,
De rain here.

***

XXVII
THE SEA HORSE

Up on the old school hill looking East,
I see a small white dot
On the deep blue sea.
It's the 'Sea Horse'
Government's ferry boat.

Travel between the capital,
Grand Turk, --- and South Caicos
Was its thrice weekly route.
Good or bad weather
Determined your experience
Of a seahorse truth.

Rocking and tossing from side to side,
Dipping and diving
And OH! … so slow …..
But if you miss that boat,
You have no other way to go.

The ride is always very rough
If you don't believe me….
Ask high school students who travelled
Often enough.

This big boat in my estimation
But, yet so small ….
Is captained by Stanley Malcolm
Who is also not so tall,
But one of TCI's best captains of all.

His skilful expertise
Causes this rocking horse
Divide that deep 'Channel' sea.
At times, the dips, dives and rolls
Makes one hold one's breath,
Closes one's eyes
Because one does not want to see
The next wave roll.

Uncle Shady, (Shadrack Grant) the first mate
Is there to comfort
Through the breaking waves.
So, what then must one do?
Loosen up and enjoy the ride.
South Caicos harbour ------
Safe and sound.

***

XXVIII
THE DONKEY CART

The donkey cart,
Back in the day
Was a very important means
Of transportation.
It served the purpose
Of today's vehicular collection.

The donkey cart –
It carried people to church
To the clinic.
And the bride and groom
After their marriage ceremony.

It took the grocery from the wharf
To every shopkeeper's door,

And from the shop to
Some people's house.

The donkey cart,
Was an integral part of the salt industry.
It carried loose salt from the ponds
Then in later years,
And bags of salt
To wharfs
To be exported.

The donkey cart, in later years of its existence, became
The water transportation.

Ba Hen and his donkey, 'Woolly Boy',
Were most famous to South Caicos residents.
Every day to the tank they went
Collected their water
And took to several homes.

At one time the donkey cart,
Was the official means of transportation
So, carrying the dead
To their resting place,
Was also a journey it had to make.

***

XXIX
BAY TANSY

It's Saturday morning
So, Bay Tansy is reigning!
No need to hide
It has nowhere going.
It will be here
Whenever you return,
So, have it now
Why everyone is getting theirs.
The sooner you have it,
The less you will get.

Bay Tansy,
That pretty, lacey
Green colour running plant
Found at the seaside
In the white sand,
Looks awesome
In white
But an excellent laxative
If you were to think twice.

Back in the day
Parents took pride in cleansing
Their children on a Saturday,
And Bay Tansy
Was the preferred bush medicine.

Very bitter tasting
If I must say,
But have it, was a must
And you had to obey.
I hated it then,
And it is worse now.
Just looking at Bay Tansy
Gives me a bad feeling.

I guess mothers passed on
What had been handed down,
But Bay Tansy for me
Died a natural death.

***

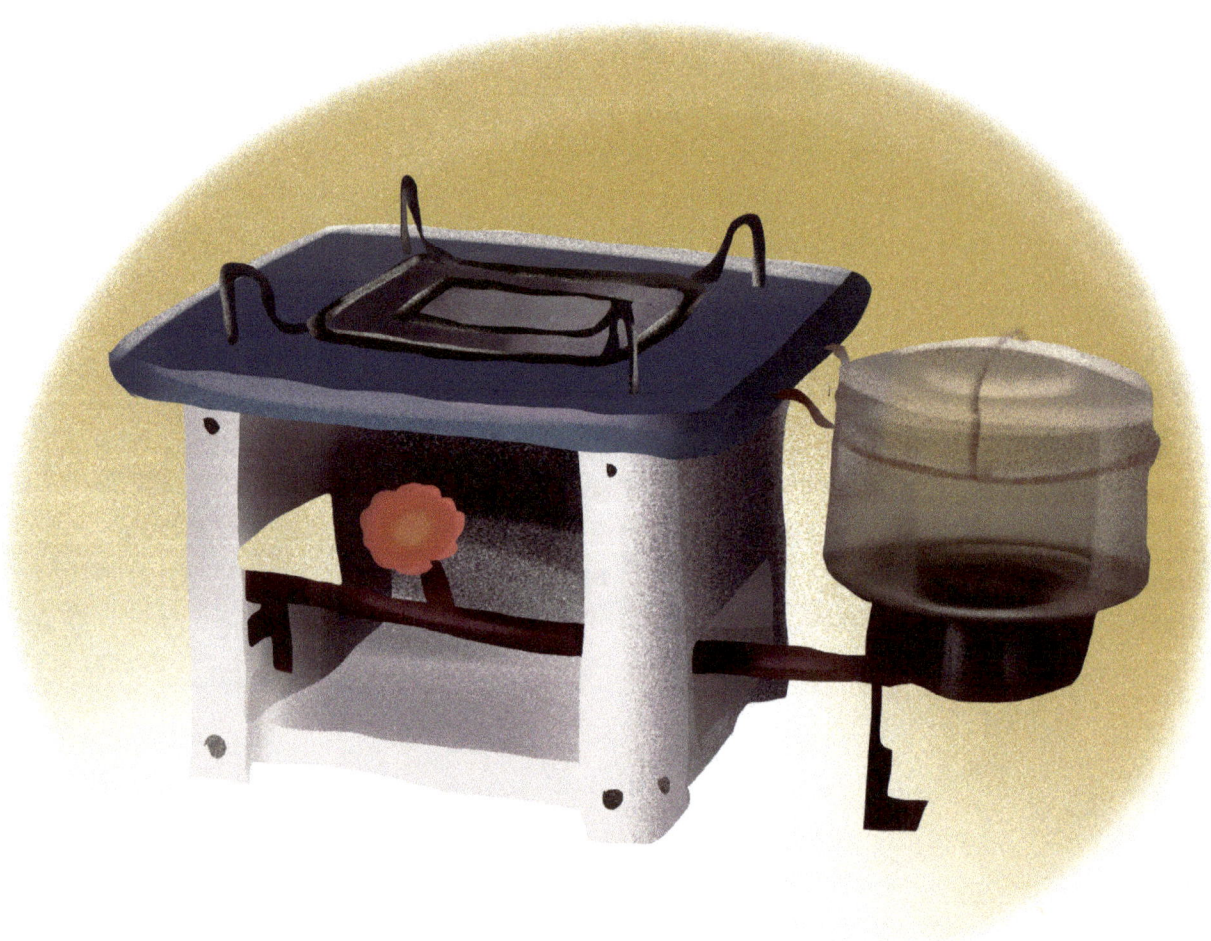

XXX
THE OIL STOVE

Yaaall still cooking on three rocks?
So, you ain't hear bout the new stoves
In the shops?
One burner,
Two burners
And even three ----
Go by Mr. Ewing's store
And you will see.

Don't let him catch you looking --------
Cause you know what that will mean,
But come back and tell your Mar,
What you have seen.

The oil stove,
Is better than wood
No more going in the bush.
Just go to Aunty Abby
And buy kerosene
She might be long in getting it
But never mine,
Let her take her time.

The oil stove is better,
No cally pots to wash -
Blacking up one's hands,
Fingernails taking forever to look right,
Don't let it get on your clothes ---
Kiss that "Good night!"

The oil stoves cannot take breeze
So be careful where you put these.
Once lit and oil flows well
Manage your gauge so that
The flame stays blue.
Food will cook
In a short time too.

***

HAITI BOAT IN ....

Haiti Boat In!
Haiti Boat In!
Full of mangras, oranges,
Pears and things.
Look! Look! Look here!
Everybody heading in town
To see wha dey can ge ----
Some things for themselves
Or some things to sell.

Baskets and baskets of produce
Are being brought from the boat to the dock,
Those little dinghies are well stock.
As they approach, the
People get closer and closer,
So, try to get close too -------
Or you will be out of luck.

Vendors from the boat
Are selling to their special customers,
So, try your best to get next
To those selling to anyone.

While all this is going on
Youngsters are rushing
On the wharf ....
Stripping to under clothes alone
Then diving overboard.

They swim to the boat
To get, 'Touched mangoes'
Thrown overboard.
These they hoard.
When they come to shore,
They might have ten or more.

***

XXXII
AUNTY FLOSSY'S DATE TREE

Who's willing to climb
Aunty Flossy's date tree?
Echoed the children
In the street.

I ain't ga climb
So high up there ----
Cause when I fall
Everybody goin disappear.

Those dates are nice but to get them
One might have to pay a price.

Many children who stayed
Under this same tree
Got their head burst

When rocks were thrown
To knock off dates
And they fell back almost in place.

You might be laughing,
But that is true.
I know about that -----
It happened to me too.

Those dates ..... Sweet and tasty.
Better than any
Bought from the factory.

We will sit and wait
Till the big boys come out to play,
They will knock them down
And we will pick up and run away.
They can't beat us running anyway.

Here they come -----
Let's gather closer to the tree
You be quick
When they give the first lick.

My 'Gumpsy!' Look at the dates, what a load,
Remember, run quick,
You don't want to get hit.
Gather your share and enjoy every bit.

***

XXXIII
ON DE BENCH

There goes Mr. Harry
Headed to his girlfriend's house.
There he will spend
The next three hours
'On De Bench'.

He's going to visit his girl friend
But can't stay until ten.
Her parents will let him know
By clearing their throat
And that means
Time up, you've got to go.

They'll sit in the same room
Where the parents or adults are
And carry on conversation
Of which all will be a part.

There'll be no touching or hugging
Not even holding hands
Adults are keeping a keen eye
On whatever goes on.

The clearing of throat has begun.
Harry knows that he must move on.
But if he chooses to ignore
An adult, the tactics will implore:
Turn the broom upside down
And pour in some salt,
Keep clearing the throat …
Longer, clearer and even more.

Harry needs to obey
If another 'On De Bench' experience
He would want to take.
An adult will walk him to the door
While his girlfriend looks on.

He leaves knowing that his time tonight has expired
He is looking forward to the next time as required
To visit and sit … 'On De Bench',
To talk to the girl, he always admired.

***

XXXIV
GATHERING FIREWOOD

Catch the donkey cart
Going in the bush,
You might have to walk back home
But at least we'll have some firewood.

They rode to Highland
The old estate in the East
Where many dead trees
And dry bush
Lay in waste.

I collected my bundle
And tied with a string
Then helped the old man
To load his cart with every other piece.

We headed back home
Uncle Harry in his cart
And I walked beside it
With my bundle on my head.

I was used to carrying wood
For my mom to use
And sometimes going to get it alone,
But this time Uncle Harry
Was good company and
We chatted about everything.
This made the journey
Seem shorter and my load lighter.

***

XXXV
DROUGHT

Although government had several water tanks
And there were a few private ones too,
Water was now getting scarce
What were the people to do?

We were having a drought.
Desperation was growing.
People asked:
Where would we get water this bout?
The answer was,
From the Dominican Republic
Without a doubt!

Water was rationed
At government tanks,
Families got a few buckets full each day
For which they used to cook and drank.

Many arose early morn
And walked or rode in donkey carts
To Basden, Highland and New wells.

They caught the flowing tide
The freshest water then
Cause it would not last too long.
This was used for washing clothes
and bathing.
Some persons stayed at the wells and washed.

One day,
The water ship came,
Children went to see
What was going on.

Water was pumped from the ship
To government tank, near Timco, in town.
The water was not clear at all
But the health inspector did his job
And purified for everyday care.

***

XXXVI
SCALE

I watched the men
As they cleaned the pond
After the salt was harvested.
They raked what was left behind
In mounds to be taken away.

This was not to be discarded,
Instead, a smooth road surface
It would make.

Heaps of salt
At the edge of the road or
Certain places on a street would be placed.
For a while
There they would stay
Until the pickle drains away.

This made the salt hard and compacted
And 'Scale' became its name.
Excellent for packing,
By flattening
On the rocky roads,
Scale gave everybody a new road.

It was best for riding bicycles,
Pushing box,
Donkey and horse carts
Since they were
The main mode of transportation.
I cannot leave out 'Walking!"
Everybody did that without complaining.

I never liked
When the road work began,
Because the Scale
Would get moistened.
To walk on it
Meant your footwear would get wet.
To wear slippers
One knew not to do that.

If slippers you did wear, you got stuck,
And to have a bruise, cut or toe jam
Pickle ... the moist liquid
Would let you know
That is never to be done.

With the passing of time and dry weather,
That slushy coloured: Pink, brown, or grey salt,
Turns white and hard
And a better road you could not find.

When the sun got very hot,
Glittering crystals of scale on the road
Made it difficult for one to see,
Just as if it blinded me.

***

XXXVII
DRIED CONCH

I ran when I reached over there
Where that big boat is.
I didn't want to smell
The fishermen conchs.

You see those sticks
Looking like a high table?
That was the conch rack
With sticks laid across the top
And spaces in between
To hold the conchs laid
Upside down
As they hung out of their shells.

As the muscles lost strength
The conch took a longer time
Getting back into its shell.
After a while it stayed hanging outside.

The fisherman robbed bay sand
On his hands
Then pulled each conch out
And did not break the shell.

The conchs were washed in the sea,
Then flattened with a bruiser,
Strung in pairs with a piece of thatch
Then thrown over a line to dry.

This did not happen overnight,
So, every morning,
They were put on the line
And every evening, taken inside.
This continued until the conchs
Were hard and dried.

It is still true to say:
Dried conch is sweeter than
The fresh conch,
It has a stronger flavour and better
Taste too!

***

COMMUNITY

XXXVIII
COMMUNITY POLICING

(This poem was written by me for the occasion and recited by Enrique Dickenson, at the official launch of the Turks and Caicos Islands Community Policing, at the Parade Ground in Grand Turk in 1998)

Community Policing!
Let down your guard.
It's time to join forces by
Lending a hand,
To preserve our land.

Don't sit idle
And stare,
Or,
Keep silent
And pretend
You don't care.

Get involved
With the happenings
In your community,
We must save our YOUTHS
From failure and crime -
Those dreadful monsters,
Are waiting -
And sure to pass by.

What did you say?

Community Policing?

Yes,
Think about what
You can do
To make your community
The safest place too.

My hat I lift ..... To this programme,
And ask all of YOU ----------
To join me, on the moving van,
As together we move
Throughout our land --------,
Holding hands
In this
Community Policing Programme.

***

XXXIX

OUR TASKS

(This poem was written in 1995 for Education Week. The theme was: 'Our Children …… Our Future')

We have a country and
Although it's small
We're a part of the big wide world.
What becomes of it
Is in our hands
Cause we're the future of this land.

The teachers, the doctors the nurses
Are we,
Politicians, firemen, garbage collectors,
Even these three.

We'll be the professionals then
Cause we're the future of this land.

Every boy and girl,
A role must play,
In making our country great
Cause, we're the future of this land.

Children must know
Things they can do
To build a bright future too.
So get on track
Look what's in your hands
Cause, we're the future of this land.

The children!
That's who we are
No doubt about it,
But the future is ours.
Let's start planning now.

Come on everybody
We've a job to do
Cause, we're the future of this land.

So, boys and girls
Listening now …. Join us
We're on a journey ------- Whoa!

Let's make our country
A better place.
This is where we want to stay,
Cause, we're the future of this land.

***

XL
RECOGNIZING ACHIEVEMENT, PROMOTING EXCELLENCE

(This poem was written for Education Week)

If one little deed should go unnoticed
Don't give up!
If in your efforts, you do fail
Don't give up!
And if you feel you can make a good grade,
Try! Don't give up!

A trial its end results
Be it great or small,
Cause it's only then, that
One finds true strength
And able to prod on.

Achievement comes in many forms:
The best resulting from Hard Work,
Accepting Challenges,
Perseverance,
Good Study Habits and
Time Management.

If you should follow, what's I've suggested;
Then EXCELLENCE would,
Reward your efforts.
To achieving anything in life
Is worth the effort when done right.
So, step up boldly and take your stand
To chart your course
In achieving EXCELLENCE!
Continuously remind yourself that,
If excellence were mine to achieve
Then with determination I will proceed:
Full speed ahead I'll begin my race
Cause EXCELLENCE states
There's no time to waste.

We'll be the professionals then
Cause we're the future of this land.

Every boy and girl,
A role must play,
In making our country great
Cause, we're the future of this land.

Children must know
Things they can do
To build a bright future too.
So get on track
Look what's in your hands
Cause, we're the future of this land.

The children!
That's who we are
No doubt about it,
But the future is ours.
Let's start planning now.

Come on everybody
We've a job to do
Cause, we're the future of this land.

So, boys and girls
Listening now …. Join us
We're on a journey ------- Whoa!

Let's make our country
A better place.
This is where we want to stay,
Cause, we're the future of this land.

***

XL
RECOGNIZING ACHIEVEMENT, PROMOTING EXCELLENCE

(This poem was written for Education Week)

If one little deed should go unnoticed
Don't give up!
If in your efforts, you do fail
Don't give up!
And if you feel you can make a good grade,
Try! Don't give up!

A trial its end results
Be it great or small,
Cause it's only then, that
One finds true strength
And able to prod on.

Achievement comes in many forms:
The best resulting from Hard Work,
Accepting Challenges,
Perseverance,
Good Study Habits and
Time Management.

If you should follow, what's I've suggested;
Then EXCELLENCE would,
Reward your efforts.
To achieving anything in life
Is worth the effort when done right.
So, step up boldly and take your stand
To chart your course
In achieving EXCELLENCE!
Continuously remind yourself that,
If excellence were mine to achieve
Then with determination I will proceed:
Full speed ahead I'll begin my race
Cause EXCELLENCE states
There's no time to waste.

It has been said many times
That achieving one's goal should be
Foremost in one's head,
But just in case this you cannot understand,
Set aside some time and plan, plan, plan.

Recognizing Achievement!
This brings .... Great Joy
But, sweeter still with
EXCELLENT PERFORMANCE!!!

***

XLI
EXPLORING NEW POSSIBILITIES

(This poem was written for Education Week in 2008)

Many, many years ago,
Imagine ……, No computers, everything had to be slow,
It was using your hands
To do everything,
To do one's own thing.
No keyboards to type,
No karaoke to help you sing.

To research homework
Time and time again,
With no internet to browse, could be a real pain.
It was the library all day and
Burning of oil almost all night
In order to get information,
It was a real fight.

To do artwork,
Was just another task
For there was no clipart.

How was life without
Text Messages,

Cell Phones
And Emails?
Sending letters and messages
Were as slow as the pace of a snail.

There was no electricity ----------
So, there were no streetlights,
No electrical appliances
Yes, life without
TV, videos, computers, webcams, phones
And the like.
Transportation by boat was the way to go,
But, today, we have faster and faster aeroplanes.

Exploring New Possibilities in a Dynamic Era?

Exploring New Possibilities in a Dynamic Era
Says, that to function in the world
You had better come on Board .....
INVESTIGATE and DISCOVER!!!

YOU, are capable of inventing
Much more in this ...YOUR ERA!

***

XLII
LOOKING BACK

(This poem was written for the Grade 6 Graduation Class of the Mary Robinson Primary School in Salt Cay, Turks and Caicos Islands in the year 1999)

Looking back at my primary years
And remembering what I did,
Makes me feel rather please
Having come so far
With not much ease.

The memories of school days
Way back to the kindergarten crew
Makes me wonder
How we ever got through.

There were the tears,
Small chairs,
Playhouse, books and toys,
Stolen lunches, cries and fights
All made our day
Just right.

Then we moved on.
Six grades in all.
Isn't that a whole lot?
Each was different
And work got harder yet.

Those days are gone
And nothing can bring them back.
Mine ---- none to regret.
School was great,
That, I never will forget!

Now, we must move on
To a higher rung,
And so, we reflect.
We cannot help ....,
But look back

Looking back
Brings me much pleasure,
Moving forward
I have much to conquer.

***

www.ingramcontent.com/pod-product-compliance
Lightning Source LLC
Chambersburg PA
CBHW051317110526
44590CB00031B/4380